Investigate

Weather and Seasons

Sue Barraclough

www.heinemann.co.uk/library
Visit our website to find out more information about Heinemann Library books.

To order:
☎ Phone 44 (0) 1865 888066

📄 Send a fax to 44 (0) 1865 314091

💻 Visit the Heinemann Bookshop at www.heinemann.co.uk/library to browse our catalogue and order online.

Heinemann Library is an imprint of Pearson Education Limited, a company incorporated in England and Wales having its registered office at Edinburgh Gate, Harlow, Essex, CM20 2JE – Registered company number: 00872828

Edited by Sarah Shannon, Catherine Clarke, and Laura Knowles
Designed by Joanna Hinton-Malivoire, Victoria Bevan, and Hart McLeod
Picture research by Liz Alexander and Rebecca Sodergren
Production by Duncan Gilbert
Originated by Chroma Graphics (Overseas) Pte. Ltd
Printed and bound in China by Leo Paper Group

ISBN 978 0 431932 74 3 (hardback)
12 11 10 09 08
10 9 8 7 6 5 4 3 2 1
ISBN 978 0 431932 93 4 (paperback)
13 12 11 10 09
10 9 8 7 6 5 4 3 2 1

British Library Cataloguing in Publication Data
Barraclough, Sue
    Weather and seasons. - (Investigate)
    551.6

A full catalogue record for this book is available from the British Library.

Acknowledgements
©Alamy pp. **14** (Blackout Concepts), **26** (Nathan Keay/SMINK, Inc.); ©Bluegreen p. **27** (Philip Stephen); ©Brand X pictures p. **4** (Morey Milbradt 2001); ©Corbis pp. **11** (Paul Hardy), **8**; ©FLPA pp. **17** (Frans Lanting), **24** (Rinie Van Muers/Foto Natura); ©Getty Images pp. **5** (Guy Bubb), **10** (Ed Darack), **12** (Kai Trikkonen), **20** (Cornelia Doerr), **21** (PhotoDisc), **23** (Jan Greune), **27** (David Woodfall); ©Imagestate p. **7**; ©PhotoDisc p. **21** (Hans Wiesenhofer), **20**; ©Photolibrary p. **16** (DFernandez & MPeck); ©Reuters p. **28**; ©Rex Features p. **15** (Bournemouth News); ©Science Photo Library pp. **9** (George Post), **13** (Bjorn Svensson), **25** (Lea Paterson), **29** (Duncan Shaw).
Cover photograph of Icicles Covering Tree Branches reproduced with permission of ©Corbis (Layne Kennedy).

Every effort has been made to contact copyright holders of material reproduced in this book. Any omissions will be rectified in subsequent printings if notice is given to the publishers.

Contents

Some words are shown in bold, **like this**. You can find out what they mean by looking in the glossary.

Weather

Weather is what is happening in the air around us.
The weather can be sunny, windy, cloudy, or rainy.
Weather can be warm, hot, or cold.

People wear different clothes for different weather. Some clothes keep us dry or warm. Some clothes protect us from the Sun.

Changing weather

The Sun, air, and water cause changes in the weather. The Sun warms Earth and this moves air and water around. This is known as the water cycle.

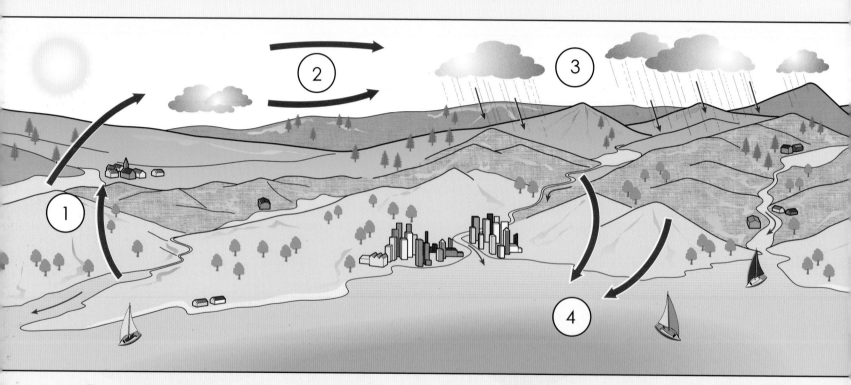

1. The Sun's heat evaporates water from sea and living things.

2. Water vapour rises and cools to form clouds.

3. Clouds are blown by the wind. They contain tiny drops of water that fall as rain or snow.

4. Water soaks into the ground or flows into rivers and lakes on its way to the sea.

The water cycle is important because it makes rain. Rain gives us clean water to drink. Plants need rain and the Sun to make food to help them grow.

Q

What are clouds made of?

Clouds are made of tiny drops of water.
The drops are so tiny they float in the air.

 Clouds can appear in many
different shapes.

Rain is made of drops of water that fall from clouds. Tiny drops of water make clouds join together. The bigger drops are too heavy to float so they fall as rain. Rain can be soft **drizzle** or it can be big, heavy raindrops.

These big, thick clouds show that a storm is on the way. Storms can bring rain, snow, or hail. Sometimes it is very windy too. The clouds can make lightning and thunder.

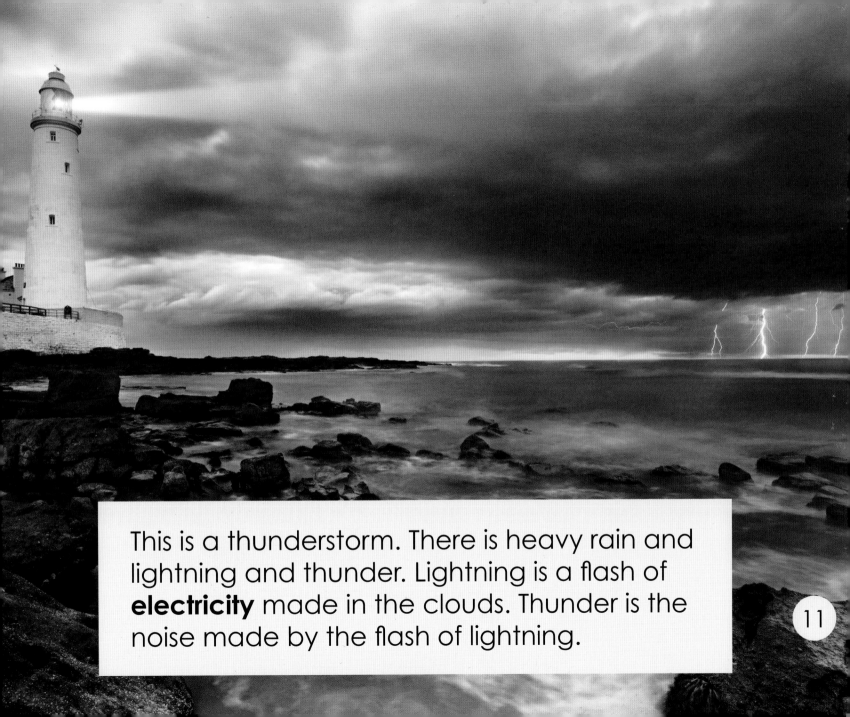

This is a thunderstorm. There is heavy rain and lightning and thunder. Lightning is a flash of **electricity** made in the clouds. Thunder is the noise made by the flash of lightning.

11

Sleet, snow, or hail can fall from the clouds when
it is cold. Sleet is icy rain. Hail is hard balls of ice.
Snow is softer flakes of ice.

Sometimes when the weather is very cold there is frost and ice. Frost and ice are frozen water.

 What type of weather is good for flying a kite?

13

A Windy weather is good for flying a kite.

Wind is moving air. The wind pushes the kite up into the sky.

14

Wind can be a gentle breeze that blows leaves from a tree. Wind can also be very strong. It can be strong enough to blow a tree over. The strongest wind is called a **hurricane**.

Cold and hot

Some parts of Earth are cold all the time. There are places at the very top and bottom of Earth called **poles**. At the poles the weather is cold and icy. Only animals that can survive in ice and snow can live there. Plants do not grow well.

Some parts of Earth are hot all the time. These places in the middle of Earth are hot and rainy all year round. Plants grow well in these warm, wet places.

 What makes parts of Earth hot?

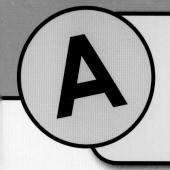

A The Sun. The Sun warms Earth and makes it hot. The Sun does not shine on some parts of Earth as strongly, so these parts are colder.

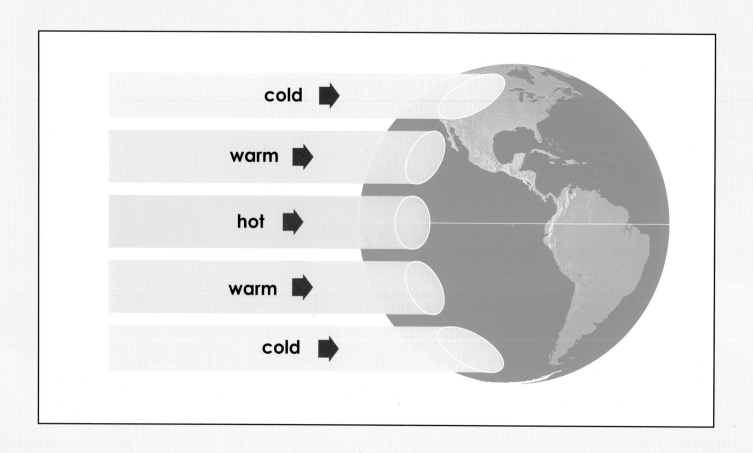

cold ➡

warm ➡

hot ➡

warm ➡

cold ➡

A **temperature** shows how hot or cold something is.
This chart shows the temperature during a year in
one part of the world.

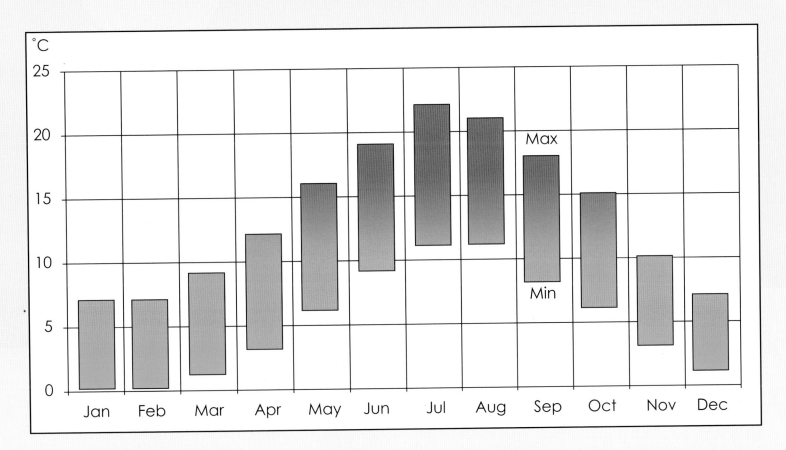

Seasons

A **season** is a time in a **year** when a type of weather usually happens. Some parts of the world have four seasons. The four seasons are spring, summer, autumn, and winter. Each season has different weather.

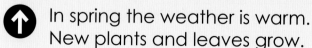 Autumn weather is cool. Trees start to lose their leaves.

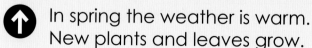 In spring the weather is warm. New plants and leaves grow.

 Summer is hot. Plants grow flowers and fruits.

 Winter is cold. The weather can be snowy and icy.

Q What causes the four seasons?

The Sun.

The Sun causes the different **seasons**.
Earth turns as it travels around the Sun.

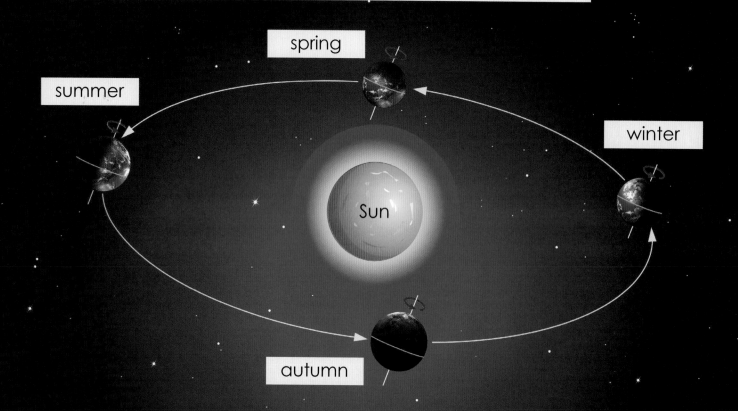

spring

summer

winter

Sun

autumn

22

In winter the weather is colder because Earth is tilted away from the Sun. As Earth moves around the Sun, the weather gets warmer.

← The Sun still shines in winter but it does not feel so warm.

Living with weather

Animals have special ways to live in very hot or cold places. Some animals have thick fur to keep them warm in cold weather. Some animals live underground to keep cool in hot weather.

This polar bear has very thick fur. ⬆

Many people who work outside need to know how the weather will change. Boats might not go out to sea if it is going to be very stormy. Farmers need to know if there will be enough rain for their plants to grow.

Q What does this weather device show?

A It shows how much rain has fallen. This device is called a **rain gauge**.

Scientists at weather stations measure how much rain falls every month. They also measure **temperature** and wind speed.

It is useful to know about dangerous weather. Big storms and strong winds can damage buildings and trees. By watching the weather carefully, scientists can guess how weather will change. They can warn us to be ready for bad weather.

The changing weather and **seasons** are important for all living things. Rain helps plants grow but too much rain can kill plants. The weather can bring blue skies or beautiful rainbows. It can also bring strong winds, storms, and floods.

↑ Floods are caused by too much rain. The water can wash away soil and knock buildings down.

The weather and seasons are important for life on Earth. We need to understand how the Sun, air, and water work together to change the weather and seasons.

Checklist

Changes in weather are caused by:
- the Sun
- air
- water.

Weather can be:
- sunny
- windy
- rainy
- snowy
- cloudy.

Cloud facts:
- Some clouds look dark and grey. This is because they are so thick the Sun cannot shine through them.
- Mist and fog are clouds that are close to the ground.

Glossary

drizzle a type of rain which is made of very small, light drops of water

electricity form of energy that makes light and heat and can make machines work

hurricane very strong wind that moves in a circle

poles parts of Earth that are furthest north or south

rain gauge a tool used to measure how much rain falls

season time in the year when a type of weather usually happens

temperature how hot or cold something is

year length of time that is 12 months (365 days) long

Index